TEN KEYS FOR UNLOCKING THE BIBLE COURSE

LEADERS' GUIDE

Colin S. Smith

MOODY PUBLISHERS
Chicago

© 2003 BY COLIN S. SMITH

Interior design by Kelly Wilson, Paetzold Associates, Inc.,
St. Charles, Illinois.

ISBN: 0-8024-6561-7

1 3 5 7 9 10 8 6 4 2

Printed in the United States of America

Leaders' Guide

INTRODUCTION

Hosting a *Ten Keys* study is an exciting way to introduce others to the Bible. You can do this either in a large-group setting or by opening your home to a small group of neighbors and friends. These notes will explain how you can make your study most effective.

OPENING THE BIBLE

Ten Keys is designed to open up the Bible to people with little or no prior knowledge of it. Mature Christians will benefit from it, but it was conceived with the beginner in mind.

When you invite people to your study, tell them it is an opportunity to understand the message of the Bible and that they do not need to have any prior knowledge or experience. Many people today know little about the Bible, but they have a general respect for it. You may be surprised at how appealing your invitation will be.

The *Ten Keys* study makes no attempt to defend the Bible or to argue that it is true. It simply explains what the Bible says in its own terms. God's Word is like living seed, and where it is sown it will bring a harvest.

BUILDING RELATIONSHIPS

Ten Keys offers the opportunity for a small group to discover the Bible together. As the leader, try to create an open atmosphere where people can freely share their own questions, issues, and insights.

Over the ten weeks of this study, group members will build trust and openness with one another that will help them in their spiritual lives. Some of their greatest insights will be gained from one another. Sharing a meal or at least a dessert together is an important part of the *Ten Keys* experience. Food fosters friendship and helps to build a sense of community.

Developing a Worldview

The *Ten Keys* study traces the Bible story from Genesis to Revelation and shows how the whole Bible points to Jesus Christ.

The Old Testament builds a framework, or worldview, in which the good news of Jesus can be understood. It begins with God telling us who He is and who we are, what our problem is, and what needs to be done to put our lives right with God. When we grasp these things, we will be in a good position to understand why we need Jesus Christ.

HOSTING A *TEN KEYS* COURSE IN YOUR HOME

Your home is a perfect environment for hosting a *Ten Keys* study. You might consider teaming up with a neighbor or friend to share the responsibilities. One person can host while the other is responsible for leading the discussion.

INVITE YOUR GROUP MEMBERS

One of the best ways to invite people to the *Ten Keys* study is to give them a copy of the *Ten Keys for Unlocking the Bible* book. This leaders' kit includes one copy and an order form to purchase additional copies at a reduced price. You can also obtain copies of the study guide for each participant. The ideal group size is between six and twelve people. If your goal is to reach seekers or beginners, it is best if most of the members of the group fit that category. Otherwise the seekers may hesitate to share the real questions and concerns they have.

If you hope to include couples with families, you will need to plan for the children. The easiest option is for couples to be responsible for finding child-care providers on their own. Another option is to simply hire a sitter to watch the kids in another part of the house. You could also recruit a few people who will run a *Ten Keys* program for the children at the same time. Ideas and lesson plans can be found on the *Ten Keys for Unlocking the Bible* web site at www.tenkeys.info.

PLAN YOUR EVENING

Here are two suggestions for structuring your time. Remember, these are just ideas. You should decide which format fits you best.

MEAL SERVED		SNACK OR DESSERT SERVED	
Meal together:	30 minutes	Conversation with beverages:	10 minutes
Setting the Scene:	5 minutes		
Video presentation:	25 minutes	Setting the Scene:	5 minutes
Discussion:	30 minutes	Video presentation:	25 minutes
		Snack/dessert served:	10 minutes
		Discussion:	30 minutes

CREATE AN INVITING ATMOSPHERE

Make sure the room is comfortable and free from distractions. Build in time to get to know one another before the actual study begins, either during the meal or over refreshments. Remind group members that discussion is an important part of the study and that you want them to feel comfortable sharing their opinions and questions.

Establish a few ground rules on the first night to foster this kind of atmosphere. We recommend these three: (1) Everyone's opinions and thoughts are valid and will be respected. (2) Nothing personal that is shared will leave the group. (3) No one needs to feel any pressure to share.

PREPARE FOR THE STUDY

In preparation for the study, preview the video and the "Following Along" section in this study guide. Try to anticipate some of the questions your group members might have. Also, look over the discussion questions beforehand. Think about *your* answers to the questions and what follow-up questions you might want to include to encourage further discussion.

BRING THE STUDY TO A CLOSE

Close your time together in prayer. Don't put anyone on the spot by expecting them to pray. As group members become more comfortable with one another, consider asking for prayer requests. Then include the requests in your closing prayer. And, of course, pray regularly for all of your group members. You may want to use a Scripture such as Colossians 1:10–11 as a guide.

You may find that participants want to hang out together after the study. This will give you an opportunity to touch base with group members to see what is on their minds. Some of your most significant conversations may come during this time or other informal conversations outside the group.

The *Ten Keys* study gives you great opportunity to help your friends and neighbors discover the life-changing message of the Bible. May God bless your study richly!

HOSTING A *TEN KEYS* COURSE IN A LARGE-GROUP FORMAT

Imagine a room filled with round tables. Animated discussions are taking place over dessert. Laughter erupts from various points in the room. At the end of the evening, people straggle out as they give hugs and handshakes to one another. A wedding reception? No, this is a picture of the large-group format in action during the *Ten Keys* study.

In the large-group format, participants sit at round tables in a larger room or hall. Each round table has a discussion leader and essentially becomes a small group during the ten weeks. A meal is served. The groups listen together to a message and then enjoy a time of discussion.

The schedule for the evening would normally be as follows:

Meal together:	*30 minutes*
"Setting the Scene" and the video message:	*30 minutes*
Discussion over dessert:	*30 minutes*

This format has proved to be very effective. The meal together adds personal camaraderie and gives participants a chance to get to know one another.

The message can be presented by video or given by someone from your church or organization.

Ideally, you want to group people at tables by their level of Bible knowledge. This helps those who are newer to the Bible to feel at ease. However, when someone invites a guest, they should be able to sit together even though they have different levels of Bible knowledge.

Develop Your Team

One of the advantages of the large-group format is that it allows people with different gifts to work together in communicating the message of Jesus Christ. Volunteers will find great joy in being part of something significant.

Your team will need to cover the following issues: Prayer, catering, greeting, childcare, aesthetics, and setup of the room. You may want to recruit one person for each of these tasks. The person will need to find others to serve with him or her.

Plan for the Children

It will be important to offer a safe, friendly, and fun option for the children if you hope to have families come to the study. The *Ten Keys for Unlocking the Bible* web site (www.tenkeys.info) offers practical ideas for running a *Ten Keys for Unlocking the Bible* program for children while the adults are meeting.

Pray for the Study

Commit your study to the Lord in prayer and pray for individual members. The *Ten Keys* web site will give you some practical ideas for developing prayer support for your study.

Recruit Your Discussion Leaders

A good discussion leader is someone who can make people feel comfortable and facilitate a lively discussion. You want to avoid someone who might dominate the conversation or lecture the participants. This is a time for self-discovery and discussion.

See the section on discussion leaders for more information on their role.

Invite Participants

One of the best ways to invite people to your *Ten Keys* study is to give them a copy of the *Ten Keys for Unlocking the Bible* book. This leader's kit includes an order form to purchase additional copies, as well as additional copies of the participant's study guide.

Most of the participants will attend the study because someone they know has invited them. Encourage your church members to step out and invite their friends to be part of the study.

RUN THE STUDY

Set the date for your course and give yourselves at least one month to invite people. See the comments under "Session-by-Session Guidance for Discussion Leaders" for more information on running your study.

YOUR ROLE AS A
DISCUSSION LEADER

Leading a *Ten Keys* study is a wonderful opportunity and a very rewarding experience. You will have the great privilege of helping others to grasp the message of the Bible and the good news of Jesus Christ.

As the discussion leader, you are responsible for establishing a positive, open atmosphere that will allow group members to learn and build relationships. Here is how you can do that.

HELPING GROUP MEMBERS FEEL COMFORTABLE

This may be the first time some in your group have ever been involved in a discussion of spiritual issues. They may be slightly uncomfortable and unsure what to expect. You can help ease their tensions and create a warm and inviting atmosphere.

Make sure everyone is introduced to each other. Watch for anyone being left out during socializing before the study and try to bring that person in. Once the formal group time begins, clearly explain how the evening will unfold.

Communicate that everyone's opinions are valued but no one is obligated to share anything. Acknowledge people's contribution and let them know that you appreciate their input.

Offering dessert during the discussion time makes the discussion more informal and provides a welcome distraction for those who are more hesitant to share.

FACILITATING A LIVELY DISCUSSION

The discussion time is very important and will largely determine how group members feel about their experience. Your role as the leader is to help your group members discover and process these truths for themselves. To accomplish this, you must ask questions and be a good listener.

Here are a couple of suggestions to encourage a lively discussion. When someone offers a short answer to a question, you may be tempted to jump in and elaborate on the answer. Instead, affirm their answer and ask them to elaborate on it. If they are hesitant, open up the opportunity to others.

Group members will often direct their answers to you as the leader, especially during your first few meetings together. Ideally, you want members to respond to one another. You can encourage this by using one of the following questions: "What do the rest of you think?" "Can somebody respond to what Joe said?" "Does anybody want to agree or disagree with what Mary said?"

Also, you need to be comfortable with a short silence after you have asked a question. Resist the temptation to fill the silence with your comments. If no one is answering, try rephrasing the question.

And take heart! As the group becomes more and more comfortable being together, your discussion will become more vibrant and stimulating.

DEALING WITH A DOMINANT PERSONALITY

Be careful not to dominate the discussion time. Your job is to ask questions, listen attentively, and encourage group members to respond to one another. You should be talking less than 25 percent of the time. The "Session-by-Session Guidance" section will give you more practical advice on facilitating a discussion.

One problem that can discourage a group is a dominant group member who monopolizes the discussion. It is your role as the group leader to address this problem. One way you can do this is to specifically call on others in the group to try and even out the discussion. It may also help to avoid eye contact with the dominant group member after asking a question.

Another option is to talk with the person outside the group time. Affirm the individual for being willing to share his or her thoughts but let the person know you are concerned that others are not entering into the discussion. Ask him or her to help you draw out the rest of the group by limiting his comments.

ENCOURAGING THE TIMID

Some group members will be more hesitant about participating in discussion than others. Don't pressurize them to contribute. Some people learn best by sitting back and taking it all in.

One way of gently drawing out quieter members of the group is to ask each member to respond to the opening question in the discussion. These questions are open-ended and there are no right or wrong answers. They offer a good opportunity for quieter members of the group to find their voice and contribute to the discussion.

Also, look for cues from quieter members. If they are leaning forward and seem to have something to say during the discussion, you might call on them and say something like, "Mary, what do you think about this?" Do this carefully, however, as you do not want to put someone on the spot. Some members are simply more comfortable listening.

GUIDING YOUR TIME TOGETHER

As the discussion leader, you are responsible for managing the time. It will be up to you to transition from the social time at the beginning to the actual study. You also want to keep the discussion on track and make sure the group ends on time. This is important for building trust. Group members want to know someone is in control, especially during the first few weeks.

SESSION-BY-SESSION GUIDANCE FOR DISCUSSION LEADERS

Session One

Since this is your first session together, take time to get to know each other before the message. Begin by asking everyone to share some basic information about themselves—where they live, what they do for a living, etc. Add a more informal question such as, "What do you like to do to relax?" or, "Where is your favorite vacation spot?" Then ask group members to share what they would like to get out of the study. This will give you a sense of people's expectations and needs and how you can tailor the course to meet their expectations.

Take a few minutes to explain the format for the evening, reminding the group that they will have an opportunity for discussion. Then read the short "Setting the Scene" section from the study guide and show the video. It is helpful to tell the group that the video runs for twenty-five minutes. If you have chosen to present the teaching material yourself, keep your presentation within this time frame.

Use the questions in the study guide for your discussion, but don't feel pressured to cover all of them. The goal is to have a lively discussion. Keep the discussion to the time you have stated. It is better to leave people wanting more than to extend the discussion until people tire of it.

After closing your time together, you can invite people to stay for more informal discussion.

End each discussion by reading the "Building the Story" point. This will reinforce the story line of the Bible. Remind the group that advance preparation is not necessary for this study but that the "Looking Ahead" section gives some direction if they would like to use it.

The *Ten Keys* study makes no attempt to defend the Bible or to demonstrate that it is true. The purpose of the study is allow the Bible to speak for itself. You may want to tell your group that the aim is not to discuss whether we can believe the Bible but to discover what it says.

Some people will have questions during session one about the truth of the Bible and Creation; during later sessions they may question evidence for the Resurrection and so forth. It is usually best to avoid making these questions the focus of discussion, but it is important to provide an answer. The *Ten Keys* web site (www.tenkeys.info) includes a range of helpful resources for answering these questions.

Session Two

Nearly everyone has heard of the Ten Commandments, but many have not thought very deeply about why these commands were given or what role they play in the Christian life.

The goal of this session is to see that God's commandments are a reflection of His own character and that they reveal our need of Jesus Christ. This can be a tough pill for us to swallow, but it is essential for understanding our need of God's grace and forgiveness.

Some members of your group may feel that they measure up pretty well to the Ten Commandments. Jesus once spoke with a man who felt this way and asked him a question that revealed his fundamental selfishness (Matthew 19:16–22). You may find it helpful to refer to this story and to the portion of the Sermon on the Mount where Jesus explains that the Law searches our attitudes as well as our actions (Matthew 5:21–30).

Questions three and four give good opportunity to probe the difficulty of keeping the commandments. As the group begins to think more deeply about the commandments, you will find that they will have a greater appreciation of how difficult they really are.

Your discussion here is important because it will help your group to understand why we need the power of the Holy Spirit in order to grow in fulfilling the law of God.

Question six moves the discussion onto our hope in Jesus Christ. No Christian ever fulfills God's Law perfectly in this life, but by the power of the Holy Spirit we are able to move in that direction and to keep growing in all that it means to live in a way that is pleasing to God.

It will be important to end this discussion on the positive note of the life that is made possible by the power of the Holy Spirit.

Session Three

The Day of Atonement is a powerful visual presentation, explaining why Jesus Christ had to die and how His death can take away our sins. This will likely be a new insight for many.

Before viewing the video, walk through the "Setting the Scene" section carefully, pausing to see if anyone has questions. Also, review the layout of the tabernacle together.

In your discussion, pay special attention to question two. You may want to walk through the five acts in the drama of the Day of Atonement and let different members discuss how they would have felt as they watched these events.

Question four may open up some widely different ideas about the appropriate way of confessing our sins. The key point to emphasize is that our sins are to be confessed to God, and that if we have offended another person, we should also confess a specific sin to that person. While it may not be possible to name all our sins, it is important to be specific in identifying and confessing particular sins and asking the forgiveness of God.

The moment when the high priest prayed, confessing the sins of the people, was especially important. If your group can grasp the concept of guilt being transferred, they will be very close to understanding why Jesus had to die, and what it means for Him to bear our sins.

The Old Testament builds a framework for understanding Christ and His mission. One participant in the *Ten Keys* study found that the connection between the Day of Atonement and Christ's death on the cross became so clear to him that he could not imagine how Jewish people today could miss it. This demonstrates the important role of the Old Testament in helping us to understand the work of Christ. This man put his faith in Christ a few weeks later.

At the end of the discussion, read the short "Building the Story" statement, and end the session with prayer. Since this is your third week together, you may like to ask if group members have any prayer requests. Lead in prayer for these yourself, making sure that you cover each one.

Session Four

This session ends with an opportunity to respond to what we have learned so far by trusting Christ as Savior. The video points out the differences among "looking," "trying," "knowing," and "buying," and includes a prayer for those who would like to receive what Christ offers. Some may be ready to make this commitment. Others will not, and it is important that nobody should feel pressured.

You might want to give people an opportunity to respond by simply saying, "What did you think?" This may lead to a fruitful discussion. If participants do not respond to that, you can simply dive into the questions.

Question five is especially important in this discussion. Many people believe that our good works play some part in our salvation. This question offers a good opportunity to open up that issue by showing that we cannot offer anything to God, and that salvation is about receiving what He offers to us.

You will notice that question six is labeled "for personal reflection," so it is important that nobody feels forced to share his or her response. You may consider asking someone who has come to know Christ as his Savior to share how he came to the place of "buying" in his own life. Make sure you ask the person in advance so he or she is not put on the spot.

If you are using *Ten Keys* in a large group format, encourage those who made a decision to follow Christ to share this with others in their group. One way of doing this is to have a response card at the table every week that participants would use to inform you if they are coming back the next week. You can encourage them to use this same card to also communicate suggestions, questions, or commitments of faith.

The outline in the workbook ends with a prayer that someone can use to receive what Christ offers. Remind the group that we can express our desire to "buy" through prayer. Tell them this prayer is a sample of the kind of prayer they could pray to express their response to God's invitation.

Session Five

Session five introduces us directly to Jesus Christ, showing that He is God, He is man, and He is holy. These truths are foundational for understanding how Jesus can bear the sin of the world and reconcile humanity to God.

Questions four, five, and six address these central issues. If Jesus was not God, He would not be in a position to reconcile us to God. Christ's love for us is God's love for us, because Jesus the Son is one with God the Father.

Remember that the aim of the *Ten Keys* study is to explain what the Bible says. It is important to emphasize that nobody can fully understand how Jesus can be both God and man. Yet this is what the Bible reveals to us about Him.

If Jesus was not man, He would not have been able to stand in our place and bear the punishment for sin on our behalf. The animals sacrificed in the Old Testament could never take away sin. All they could do was illustrate the principle that a life had to be laid down. But it had to be a human life that was laid down for the sin of humanity.

The holiness of Jesus is our third learning point in this session. If Jesus had any sins of His own, He would not have been able to bear the sins of others. So the holiness of Jesus is of great importance. He is unlike any other person who has ever lived. He alone is God, man, and holy, and so He is uniquely qualified to take away the sins of the world.

Question seven is offered for personal reflection. Depending on the dynamics of your group and your experience last time, you could give participants an opportunity to share their answers if they feel comfortable.

Session Six

Session six brings us to the heart of the Christian faith as we explore the significance of Jesus' death on the cross.

This presentation builds on important truths learned in the earlier sessions, showing how the story of God diverting the curse onto the ground in the Garden of Eden and onto the goat on the Day of Atonement was fulfilled as God diverted the judgment for our sins onto Jesus.

We also follow the story of the thief on the cross, tracing the five steps by which he came to trust in Jesus. These five steps are then offered at the end of the session as an opportunity for members of your group to consider where they are in relation to Jesus Christ and to take that final step of placing their trust in Him.

The video presentation ends with an opportunity for reflection and a prayer of response. Take the lead by closing your eyes as an example or give the group a cue, such as, "Let's close our eyes and follow along with the video."

This session is a good point to check in and see how participants are progressing on their spiritual journey. For the large-group setting, you will want to provide a nonthreatening way for participants to share with you if they have come to the point of trusting Christ.

For more information as to how you might follow-up with someone who indicates a commitment to Christ, see the *Ten Keys* web site at www.tenkeys.info.

In a small-group setting, look for opportunities to touch base with participants either in the informal time after the study or outside the meeting time. After the final *Ten Keys* session, you will ask participants to fill out a feedback form. This will give you another opportunity to see how the study has impacted the spiritual lives of those involved.

Session Seven

The last four sessions of our study deal with the Christian life and give a taste of the life promised to every believer in heaven. Participants will find this message encouraging, and it will likely give them a new perspective on life after death.

Remember that our purpose in the *Ten Keys* study is to present the story of the Bible in its own terms. The focus of this session is on the story of the women discovering the empty tomb, and the significance of the resurrection of the Lord Jesus Christ for us.

Some participants may be interested in exploring evidence for the Resurrection. You will find suggested resources for further study at the *Ten Keys* web site (www.tenkeys.info).

The apostle Paul recognized that the Resurrection is central to the Christian faith. *"For if the dead are not raised, then Christ has not been raised either. And if Christ has not been raised, your faith is futile; you are still in your sins"* (1 Corinthians 15:16–17). You may want to use this Scripture to enhance the discussion of question three. You could look up the verse and ask your group if they agree with the apostle Paul.

Most people believe in some form of life after death, but many imagine it to be something less that the life that we experience here. In the Bible it is clearly more. "To . . . be with Christ . . . is better by far" (Philippians 1:23). You may find it helpful to prompt the group's imagination by asking them what life would be like if our world was without evil, sickness, and temptation. Remind the group that the best joys of life on this earth are only a taste of what God is preparing for His people.

Question five gives an opportunity to emphasize the uniqueness of Christ. Other religions set out a system of beliefs and a way of life. Christianity is about a Person who is able to bring us into eternal life. The risen Lord Jesus Christ invites us to believe in Him and to follow Him.

Session Eight

Session eight tells the story of Pentecost and is especially important for people who have come to believe in Jesus but still have the sense that the Christian life is making an effort to live a better life.

The Holy Spirit indwells and empowers all believers. This is a wonderful truth but one that many find difficult to grasp. Some see the Holy Spirit as an impersonal source of power that we can tap into in order to accomplish our goals. This could not be further from the truth.

The Holy Spirit is the third person of the Godhead. He lives within us and empowers us to accomplish the will of God. The first two questions in the discussion will lead to a discussion of who the Holy Spirit is and will provide an opportunity to clear away confusion.

The central aim of this session is to show that God wants to use every believer to advance His purpose in some way. Every believer is gifted and empowered by the Holy Spirit for ministry. Coming to faith in Christ is the beginning of a life of discipleship and service lived out in the power of the Holy Spirit.

Question six gives an opportunity to affirm gifts that God has given to different members of the group. This discussion can be a time of great encouragement. If there are members of your group who have come to faith recently or through the study, it will be important to affirm the work of the Holy Spirit in their lives and help them see how God can use them.

With only two more sessions left after this one, you should consider providing a next step for participants should they be interested in further study after this course. There are a number of options. *Ten Keys for Unlocking the Bible* is based on the larger four-volume series *Unlocking the Bible Story*, which takes you through the Bible in much greater detail. Study guides are available to take a small group through each Testament in one year. See the web site (www.tenkeys.info) for details and additional options.

Session Nine

Session nine gives another opportunity for participants to consider where they are in their spiritual journey. We are introduced to three characters. Two of them, Hostile and Helpless, represent people who have not grasped what it means to be a Christian.

"Hostile," as the name suggests, is someone who is fundamentally antagonistic towards God. It is unlikely that someone who is hostile would be part of your group, but it is possible.

"Helpless" represents the person who would like to live a life that is pleasing to God but finds that he or she is not able to do so. You may find a number in your group who feel that this is their position.

This session provides a great opportunity to talk about the realities of the Christian life. It is important both to acknowledge the difficult struggle that we all face and to affirm the power of the Holy Spirit to lead us into victory.

The key teaching point in this session is that the Christian life is a winnable war by the power of the Holy Spirit given to every believer. It is about God's making possible what we could not do alone.

Participants should not be pressured to share which of the characters they identify with, but you can offer the opportunity for them to do so if they would like to.

The video presentation ends with a prayer that could be offered by somebody who identifies with any one of the three characters. This gives an opportunity for every member of the group to respond in some way.

Question four provides a good opportunity for the group to express how a person becomes a Christian. Remember that the difference between Helpless and Hopeful is that Helpless is simply making a personal effort to live a more moral life. He says nothing about Christ, and he knows nothing about the Holy Spirit. He is not a Christian. Trusting in Christ and living in the power of the Holy Spirit are the twin towers of the Christian life.

Session Ten

The *Ten Keys* study ends with a glimpse of what lies ahead for every Christian believer in the presence of God. The video presentation shows how the good gifts enjoyed by Adam and Eve in the Garden of Eden are moved to a new level in God's new creation.

The key teaching points are, first, that the gates to God's new city are open, and that God invites all people to come, and, second, that those who come through faith in our Lord Jesus Christ are blessed.

Use the first half of your discussion time to respond to the presentation. Heaven is a wonderful destiny to ponder! The first two questions will help to stimulate your discussion.

In the remaining time, give group members a sense of closure by allowing them to share what they have learned and how the study has impacted them. Questions four and five relate to this portion of your discussion. Participants will likely have some moving and encouraging things to say.

You may want to spend a few minutes exploring interest in another study, or consider having a group reunion in a few weeks. Group members will enjoy the opportunity to keep in touch with one another.

Before your group members leave, have them fill out the feedback form (*page 109 of the Participant Guide*), tear it out, and leave it with you. This will help you to see how the study has affected them and gauge the interest in a future study.

During the past ten weeks you have planted the living seed of the Word of God in the lives of your group members. Follow that sowing with prayer, and look to God to raise a harvest from what you have sown. Remember that, in the Lord, your labor is never in vain (1 Corinthians 15:58)!

Sɪɴᴄᴇ 1894, Moody Publishers has been dedicated to equip and motivate people to advance the cause of Christ by publishing evangelical Christian literature and other media for all ages, around the world. As a ministry of the Moody Bible Institute of Chicago, proceeds from the sale of this book help to train the next generation of Christian leaders.

If we may serve you in any way in your spiritual journey toward understanding Christ and the Christian life, please contact us at www.moodypublishers.com.

"All Scripture is God-breathed and is useful for teaching, rebuking, correcting and training in righteousness, so that the man of God may be thoroughly equipped for every good work."

—*2 Tɪᴍᴏᴛʜʏ 3:16, 17*

MOODY
PUBLISHERS
THE NAME YOU CAN TRUST®